W9-DIN-873

TORONTO

WENDY AND JACK MURPHY

GREAT CITIES

APR   2003

A BLACKBIRCH PRESS™ BOOK

THE ROSEN PUBLISHING GROUP, INC.

Published by Blackbirch Press™ in conjunction with The Rosen Publishing Group, Inc.
29 East 21st Street, New York, NY 10010
©1992 Blackbirch Press™ a division of Blackbirch Graphics, Inc.
First Edition

Printed in Hong Kong
Bound in the United States of America

Editors: Kailyard Associates
Art Director: Cynthia Minichino
Maps: Robert Italiano
Photo Research: Photosearch, Inc.

Library of Congress Cataloging-in-Publication Data

Murphy, Jack (Jack J.)
   Toronto/Jack and Wendy Murphy.
   (Great cities)
   "A Blackbirch Press book."
   Includes bibliographical references and index.
   Summary: Describes the history, people, and sights of
Toronto, a city that represents the commercial, industrial, and
financial center of Canada.
   ISBN 0-8239-1214-0
   1. Toronto (Ont.)—Geography—Juvenile literature. 2. Toronto
(Ont.)—History—Juvenile literature. [1. Toronto (Ont.)
I. Murphy, Wendy B. II. Title. III. Series: Great cities (New
York, N.Y.)
F1059.5.T684M87 1991
971.3'541—dc20   91-4173
                                CIP
                                AC

pages 4–5
The skating rink at City Hall lights up the night as citizens enjoy a Toronto winter evening.

CONTENTS

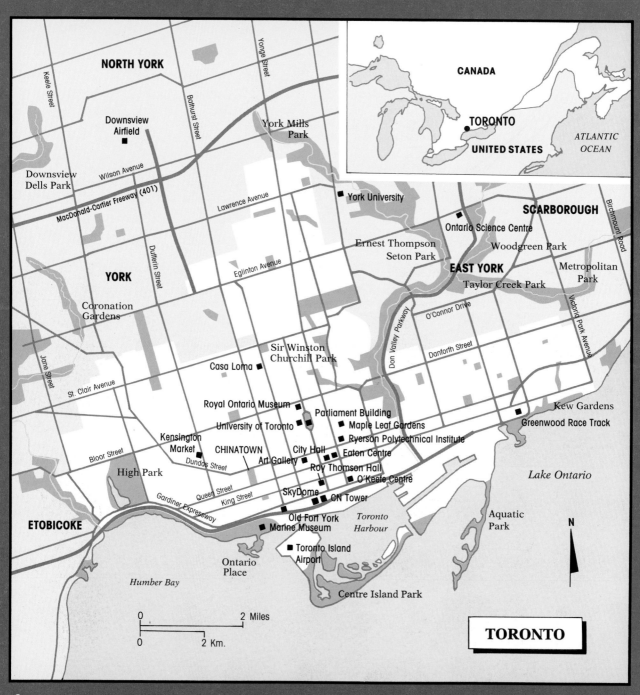

THE CITY DIRECTORY

Population: 3,800,000 (Metropolitan Toronto)

Size: 241 square miles (624 square kilometers)

Ethnic Makeup: Americans, British, Chinese, Estonians, Hungarians, Italians, Latin Americans, Polish, Portuguese, Vietnamese, Jamaicans, Japanese, and many others

City Mascot: Black Squirrel

Nickname: Hogtown

Motto: Industry, Intelligence, Integrity

Economy: The commercial, industrial, and financial center of Canada

Modern skyscrapers dominate the skyline of downtown Toronto.

THE
PLACE

"Toronto is a city that works."
      —Social Scientist Anthony Astrachan

Toronto is famous for its exciting mix of cultures, great prosperity, and its lack of the problems that trouble most other cities.

Toronto is the largest, wealthiest, and fastest growing city in Canada. It is the major city in Ontario, a province that outstrips the state of Texas in size by nearly 150,000 square miles. When people talk about Toronto nowadays, they generally mean Metropolitan Toronto. This comprises six separate areas—the City of Toronto, population approximately 612,000, together with suburban North York, Scarborough, Etobicoke, York, and the borough of East York. Together, they function as a single political unit.

Metropolitan Toronto owes its considerable good fortunes to its location. It is situated on the southern border of Canada at the western end of Lake Ontario and on the busy 2,369 mile long St. Lawrence Seaway. It also boasts a fine natural harbor formed by a collection of barrier islands.

These physical features have made the city a prime location for management, transportation, and cultural activities. Toronto is also well situated to do business with the United States: it is just 90 miles from the New York State border and just a one hour flight from 60 percent of the U.S. population.

In addition, Toronto has easy access to the major share of the country's natural resources and its most diversified industrial operations. This is due to Toronto's proximity to the Canadian Shield, or Laurentian Highlands. A vast, relatively wild and rugged high plateau of ancient granite, the Shield has pro-

The twentieth-century architecture that makes up most of the city gives Toronto a very modern feeling. Here, citizens enjoy Nathan Phillips Square in front of City Hall.

vided a historic barrier to settlement in much of Canada's north. It is rich in forests, hydroelectric (water) power, furs, and valuable ores. Its wealth of minerals include rich veins of gold, silver, nickel, cobalt, zinc, copper, iron, and uranium. Settlers, miners, foresters, and business people have exploited these resources over the centuries. And Toronto has come to play a large role as a processor, shipper, and investor in these enterprises.

An Ancient Sea

   The city itself sits in an area called by geologists the Southern Ontario Lowlands. It is a very flat expanse of land that rises from the lake shore to 300 feet at its highest altitude. These lowlands were created millions of years ago during the middle Paleozoic period. North America's climate was tropical then, and a vast body of water, known today as the Tippecanoe Sea, covered much of the continent's central region. The sea, which vanished long ago, included in its area the site now occupied by Toronto and the vast region around it. So the

The city of Toronto boasts one of the finest systems of highways and public transportation in North America.

Business and cultural activities keep
city lights burning through the night.

land under the city is actually ancient sea bottom.
Indeed, Lake Ontario is but a tiny piece of that ancient sea.

Retreating glaciers later deposited fertile soil in the
region and made it good for farming. This made the
southern part of Ontario distinctly different from the
rugged lands to the north. To this day, the country-
side around Toronto has many fine stands of decidu-
ous (leaf-bearing) trees, as distinct from the conifer-
ous (evergreen) trees in much of the rest of Canada.

Toronto's three major rivers—the Don, the Humber, and the Rouge—are important parts of the city's geography.

Ontario's maples, in particular, create the beautiful crimson colors that make Toronto's autumn season so spectacular.

Toronto's name, which is of Native American origin, means "a place of meeting." Long before the arrival of European settlers, the site was a rendezvous for neighboring tribes. They found it a convenient departure point for a portage (an overland route between canoeing waters) between Lake Ontario and Lake Huron.

The Importance of Rivers

Today, rivers play a major role in making the city a transportation hub and a place easy to reach by land and water. The rivers include the Don on the eastern side of Toronto, the Humber on the western side, the Rouge, and the Niagara River, located almost due south across Lake Ontario partly in U.S. territory. When the St. Lawrence Seaway opened to seagoing vessels in 1959, it joined the farthest of the Great Lakes and the St. Lawrence River. A single water-way then linked Canada's interior with the Atlantic Ocean, year-round. Toronto possessed a natural harbor on this waterway, which played a key role in making the city a major seaport for world shipping.

Toronto's geographic location is latitude 43° 40' North, longitude 79° 23' West, which puts it deep within the continent, a factor that might tend to give it a very harsh climate. But Lake Ontario provides a moderating influence, making Toronto not much colder in winter or warmer in summer than Boston, Massachusetts. Toronto receives an average of 54 inches of snow per year and has an average mean temperature in January of about 30.1° F (-1.1° C). In July the average mean temperature is about 80.3° F (26.8° C). Winds off the lake make the city rather humid much of the year.

THE
PAST

"The city's site was better calculated for a frog pond than for the residence of human beings."
—General Simcoe, founder of the first permanent English settlement

King Street West, near Yonge Street, around the turn of the century

The earliest known inhabitants of southern Ontario and the Toronto area were the Native North American peoples of the Huron, Iroquois, Petun, and Erie nations. All lived in relatively settled farming societies on cleared portions of the forested lowlands along Lake Ontario. Hunting groups of the Algonkin, Ojibwa, and Cree nations also passed through the region on their hunting rounds.

The arrival of European settlers forever disrupted the Indian's way of life and laid the foundation for a bitter rivalry between English and French settlers to gain control of the region. Some tension continues right to this day, visible in the uneasy relationships between their descendants. English-speaking and French-speaking Canadians prefer to live largely separate cultural and political lives, despite the fact that all of them share a single federal government.

The "capital," so to speak, of English-speaking Canada is Toronto, where the majority of the population has been traditionally of English descent. The "capital" of French-speaking Canada is the sophisticated and energetic city of Montreal, in Quebec Province. The tension between the two population centers can be seen in the constant efforts at political separation by some Quebecers. The Sovereigntists, as they are sometimes called, seek complete independence from Canada and all other countries.

Early French Settlements

The roots of this national rivalry go back to the year 1497. That is when John Cabot of England, while surveying the New World's fishing grounds, sailed into the harbor of what is now called St. John's, Newfoundland, on the Atlantic. Cabot claimed the site and all the land beyond it for King Henry VII of England. Fishing was the chief interest

This engraving shows John Cabot arriving with his son Sebastian on the shores of what is now Newfoundland.

JACQUES CARTIER
·D'APRÈS· L'ORIGINAL· DE· St· MALO·

20

of the time, and Cabot found more than enough fish for future settlers. Satisfied with this situation, the English did nothing at the time to colonize the interior or solidify their claim.

When Frenchman Jacques Cartier explored the Gulf of St. Lawrence and erected a cross on the shore of eastern Quebec in 1534, no one in England seemed to notice. And when the French attempted a settlement at Port Royal, in what is now Nova Scotia, this too went uncontested.

In a few short years, the French had established several footholds in eastern Canada. French strategy was to spread their influence across an enormous geographic area so they could eventually claim the region as a possession of France. Their interest was in land rather than fisheries, and it soon became apparent that Canada's forests were a rich source of goods for the international fur trade. The French established the city of Quebec on the north bank of the St. Lawrence River as their trading hub in 1608. Then they began aggressively establishing settlements throughout the region. Étienne Brûlé, a young Frenchman, was the first French fur trader to live among the Native Americans as a kind of government agent or *coureur de bois* (woods runner). He was also the first to take note of the fine harbor at Toronto, around 1615.

In 1627, the French began a program of transporting and resettling farmers from the French provinces

(Opposite page)
French explorer Jacques Cartier sailed into the Gulf of St. Lawrence in 1534, and claimed much of the territory for France.

of Brittany and Normandy. These peasant farmers, or *habitants*, began to take up residence in and around the region that would become the province of Quebec.

French dominion over the larger territory became a reality in 1663. King Louis XIV of France formally established the royal province of New France with its own governor and a capital at Quebec City. With royal support, French explorers and Roman Catholic missionaries forged into the interior and descended the Mississippi River to its mouth.

The English, meanwhile, were living mostly in scattered Atlantic coastal communities in what are now known as the Maritime Provinces. But their

North American Indians such as the Huron, Tobacco, and Erie, were the earliest known inhabitants of the Ontario region.

Both French and English pioneers settled many towns and villages in the Ontario territories during the 1600s and 1700s. Simple wooden houses enclosed by split-rail fences were the common architecture of these settlers.

government was no longer willing to let French ambitions go unchallenged. In 1670, they embarked on new policies designed to establish a Canada that was English and Protestant. In that year, Charles II of England granted a monopoly charter to the Hudson's Bay Company, a group of royal investors. The Company's agents began strongly challenging the French for control of Western fur trade.

France Loses Its Territory

With the outbreak of the lengthy French and Indian Wars (1689-1763), waged in Europe and North America between France and Britain, the struggle for Canada came to a head. In 1759, generals Wolfe of Britain and Montcalm of France met and died in combat on the Plains of Abraham above Quebec. When the battle was over, England was victorious.

The French and Indian Wars pitted Britain against France in a battle for control of Canada. France's General Montcalm (shown center) was killed on the battlefield just before England won its decisive victory.

The Treaty of Paris in 1763 spelled the end of
New France, and French territory was surrendered
to England. At the same time, the treaty established
the British Crown's dominion over what would
become Canada.

Toronto's own history, not surprisingly, is very
much entwined with all these developments. Around
1750, the French established a mission, fur trading
post, and fort at the foot of what is now Toronto's
Dufferin Street. They called it Fort Rouille, after its
chief commanding officer. The fort was small, but
rather than let the British seize it in 1759 (during the
French and Indian Wars), the French troops burned
it down before leaving.

Four years later, when the war ended, the sparsely
settled region around Fort Rouille became the sover-
eign territory of the British Crown. However, the
British did little at first to take advantage of their
newly won territory. They were busy trying to control the 13 unruly colonies to the south. The French
who were already in the region continued to live
according to their French-Canadian traditions.

This state of affairs changed dramatically following England's defeat in the American Revolution.
Those English colonists who had remained loyal to
the king of England were uneasy about their role in
the now independent United States. Quite sensibly,
they looked north for refuge. About 40,000 United
Empire Loyalists, as they called themselves, resettled

in Canada. Most of them took up residence in the newly created colony called Upper Canada, the future Ontario. The French majority lived chiefly around Quebec, Montreal, and Atlantic Canada, and numbered perhaps 65,000. They became part of a second colony: Lower Canada. Though subject to English rule, they were in all other respects a nation unto themselves. Great Britain, unwittingly, had created a situation in which separate English and French provinces could evolve along different ethnic, cultural, and political lines. And each province had relatively little contact with its neighbor.

The First Permanent English Settlement

The first permanent English settlement at Toronto, named York, was established in 1793. Sir John Graves Simcoe, lieutenant governor of Upper Canada, chose old Fort Rouille as the site for his new Fort Toronto and the surrounding land as the place for a permanent capital. The land, 14 miles along the Lake Ontario shorefront and 30 miles deep, was bought from the Missisauga Indians for the sum of 10 shillings.

Simcoe called the new capital "York," after the son of George III, reigning king of England, though he privately thought the place somewhat less than kingly. He described it as "better calculated for a frog pond or a beaver meadow than for the residence of human beings."

The first permanent English settlement at Toronto was founded in 1793 and was named York.

General John Graves Simcoe helped to found the earliest settlements in what is now Toronto and was the region's first governor.

Despite his misgivings, Simcoe proved an energetic administrator and a forceful personality. He wasted no time establishing English legal and governmental systems in his part of Canada. Simcoe also saw to the building of many roads, using military labor to do much of the work. Yonge Street, still a major thoroughfare in Toronto, started out as a trail cut by Simcoe's soldiers to link York's waterfront with Lake Simcoe, about 40 miles north. The governor also set up a system of generous land grants that favored the "well-affected and respectable classes," along the lines of aristocratic England. The governor hoped to create a land-owning upper class for Ontario.

But there were not nearly enough of these people to fill his huge province. Simcoe feared that failure to populate Canada would almost certainly mean eventual annexation by the much larger and more powerful United States. His solution was to coax thousands of less-favored Americans across the border with offers of free land. Between 1791 and 1812, the population of Upper Canada grew dramatically to 90,000, as Simcoe managed to give away and settle some 5 million acres of land.

The War of 1812

Tensions between the United States and Canada reached a climax in the War of 1812. The United States initiated the conflict over a host of issues, but certainly high on its list were plans for further U.S. expansion. To many, Canada seemed ready for the taking. Ex-president Thomas Jefferson wrote confidently in 1812 that "the acquisition of Canada this year, as far as the neighborhood of Quebec, will be a mere matter of marching, and will give us experience for attack on Halifax the next, and the final expulsion of England from the American continent."

This engraving shows American General Perry during his victory on Lake Erie in the War of 1812. The war was fought between America and Canada when Thomas Jefferson attempted to seize control of Canadian territory.

U.S. General Zebulon Pike led one of the few successful assaults against forces loyal to Canada during the War of 1812.

American confidence was based in part on the fact that the British were deeply engaged in fighting Napoleon and his French armies overseas. This left Britain few military resources to spare in protecting Canada. But many Americans also believed that Canada's Loyalists, if given a chance, would readily defect from support of their government and come to the aid of the American invaders.

As it turned out, the U.S. government had miscalculated. Not only was Canadian resistance far stronger than imagined, there was considerable opposition to the war in some U.S. states that favored defensive action when necessary but did not want to commit money to support offensive adventures. During the first year of the War of 1812, the Americans found themselves losing more often than winning. But then, in April 1813, the United States launched a combined military and naval assault against Fort York, which was manned by some 600 British troops.

The attack, mounted with 1,700 American soldiers, ended with the surrender of Fort York. The British militia fought hard, however, and before they surrendered they blew up the fort, killing 38 and wounding 222 of the enemy, including U.S. commander General Zebulon Pike, of Pike's Peak fame. (Other versions of the battle state that the explosion was the inadvertent result of a powder magazine that caught fire.)

   The invaders finished off their work by setting the
torch to York's government houses. The war ended
shortly after, with the boundaries between the two
countries established more firmly than before. Happily for Canada, any doubts about the loyalties of the
new Canadians, who had remained steadfast, were
set aside once and for all.

   York was rebuilt almost immediately after peace
was declared. From 1815 to 1841, it was the seat of
a provincial government led by a handful of families
and the Anglican Church. Known as the Tory Family
Compact, this elite group made virtually all decisions
affecting the financial and political life of the province to suit their own interests. Canada's parliamen-
tary system and the Compact's tight control over
who was elected excluded most ordinary folks from
participating in their own affairs. Resentment grew,
and soon a leader of disaffected citizens emerged.
He was a fiery, red-headed Scotsman named William
Lyon Mackenzie. Mackenzie had emigrated to
Toronto in 1820, and shortly thereafter began publishing a newspaper. His publication, *The Colonial
Advocate,* criticized the existing political system.

   In the same years that Mackenzie was beginning to
find support for government reform, the town of
York became a city of more than 9,000 people. At
the same time, it was changed permanently back to
the Indian name, "Toronto." In 1834, Mackenzie
was elected Toronto's first mayor. His impressive

talent for stirring the public against governmental injustices led Compact leaders to desperate measures. To curb his activities, they sent thugs to his newspaper to shut it down. Repeatedly, the bullies smashed Mackenzie's presses, threw his printing press type into Lake Ontario, and beat him up. But still the Scotsman would not be silenced.

When he became convinced that peaceful reform was fruitless, Mackenzie and his supporters turned to armed revolt. In December 1837, more than 800 Torontonians, most carrying nothing more effective than pitchforks, followed Mackenzie down Yonge Street to assemble at Montgomery's Tavern (still standing) for a takeover of Toronto. The majority were quickly scattered by government forces, but the most determined of the rebels made their retreat to fortified Navy Island, near the Niagara River. There, the army followed them and attacked again. The rebels' only supply ship was loosed from its moorings and sent to its destruction over Niagara Falls. Mackenzie was forced to flee into American territory, where he was briefly imprisoned for violating U.S. neutrality.

Mackenzie's efforts were not in vain, however. The British government became concerned about the unrest—a second revolt of French Canadians took place in Quebec over similar issues in the weeks following. In 1838, John George Lambton, Earl of Durham, was sent to Canada by Queen Victoria's

A Toronto fish market on the banks
of Lake Ontario in 1840

government to investigate. Lambton's sympathetic *Report on the Affairs of British North America* earned him the name "Radical Jack." More significantly, it led to the dismantling of the Family Compact and the introduction of many of the democratic reforms Mackenzie had called for. By 1848, representative government had come into being. (Mackenzie's grandson, W. L. Mackenzie King, would carry on the family's tradition of political activism, distinguishing himself as Canada's prime minister in the twenties, thirties, and forties.)

The City Grows

Meanwhile, the city of Toronto was growing due to a flood of newcomers. In the early decades of the nineteenth century the British government had instituted a policy of "assisted emigration." Thousands of farmers were forced to move to Canada to reduce unemployment and a series of farm crises plaguing the north of England. The lives of these involuntary settlers were difficult at best, even though they were lucky enough to find their way to a place as civilized as Toronto.

As one settler, Susanna Moodie, recorded, "Few educated persons accustomed to the refinement and luxuries of European society ever willingly relinquish those advantages. Emigration may generally be regarded as a severe duty performed at the expense of personal enjoyment." Anna Jameson found the place "like a fourth-rate or fifth-rate provincial town, with pretensions of a capital city. Toronto is . . . worse and better than other small communities—worse in so much as it is remote from all the best advantages of a high state of civilization, while it is infected by all its evils, all its follies, and better because, besides being a small place it is a young place." In spite of her reservations, Jameson thought she saw possibilities for Toronto's future: "It must advance—it may become the thinking head and beating heart of a nation, great, wise and unhappy—who knows?"

Downtown Toronto, around 1847

A New Quality of Life

Community leaders gradually succeeded in bringing a few improvements in street building and services. Roads, alternately muddy and dusty, were turned into streets, which took the punch out of the old local joke about picking a hat off the ground and finding a horse and rider under it. Plank sidewalks were laid along some of the finer streets. And in the 1840s, the first sewers and gas lines were installed under the direction of John George Howard, the first city surveyor.

In 1849, a major fire wiped out much of the old downtown, but it was quickly rebuilt. The 1850s saw the arrival of the railway, which connected the city to both Atlantic and Pacific ports and the United

States. The first steam engine built in Canada was constructed at Good's Foundry in Toronto. Named "Toronto," it made its first run to Aurora, Ontario, 25 miles to the north, in April 1853. Three years later the Grand Trunk line linking Montreal and Toronto was completed. Toronto got its first horse-drawn streetcars in 1861.

In 1868, Timothy Eaton opened a dry goods store, T. Eaton and Company, in town. It offered a number of radical new sales techniques—including fixed

Railroads came to Toronto in the 1850s. Here, citizens celebrate the launching of the Ontario, Simcoe, and Huron Railroad in 1855.

prices and customer refunds—that would soon become a model of department store management everywhere.

Canada as a whole was growing, and coast-to-coast settlement of the country had become a reality. Thanks to a continuing stream of immigrants largely from Great Britain, Canada West's population had soared to 950,000 by 1851; Canada East's population was 890,000. Strategically located to benefit from the boom, Toronto was fast rising to the status of a major commercial and industrial center. The city soon rivaled Montreal, which had been the principal city in Canada for nearly 200 years. Toronto was also growing as a banking, financial, and marketing center. Many of the English-speaking majority hoped to see it become the national capital when the provinces finally joined together. But rivalries between the English and French, and between the Protestants and Catholics, made the choice certain to be controversial.

Toronto's population was heavily weighted with Protestant Irish from the northern Irish province of Ulster. They so dominated local politics that most mayors for the remainder of the century were Protestant Irish. Strongly Calvinist and conservative in their views, the Protestant Irish influenced Toronto life and culture through membership in the Orange Order. This was an organization devoted to upholding "the moral character" of the community.

Toronto Street as it appeared in the late 1800s

Orangemen made it very clear that they were opposed to equal status for both the French and the Catholics.

They also kept a close watch on Toronto's social life, enacting a wide range of restrictive "blue laws" and "Sunday laws." These laws earned Toronto its nineteenth-century nickname, "Toronto the Good." The Order tolerated little in the way of public entertainment, night life, or any goings-on that were not strictly according to Calvinist principles. It was at one time illegal to sell candy on Sundays. This day also meant no dancing, no drinking of alcohol, and no parties of any sort. And one street in town, Temperance Street, was made off-limits for taverns.

The Dominion of Canada Is Born

On July 1, 1867, a new chapter opened in the history of Canada and Toronto: the provinces joined in a formal confederation, to be known collectively as the new Dominion of Canada. Some historians suggest that the Canadians wanted to form their own government because of the Union victory in the U.S. Civil War two years earlier. With the United States once again unified and growing, it was feared that Canada's divided provinces might be absorbed by American expansionism. Confederacy seemed the best answer to preserving Canadian independence.

Canada, for the first time, had its own written constitution. The constitution spelled out a system of government similar to that in the English-speaking mother country of Great Britain. It was complete with a parliament, a cabinet, and a prime minister. The choice for a national capital was still to be decided, and in the end Toronto was passed over. The final choice was Queen Victoria's, who decreed the little town of Ottawa as the new capital. As it had been in earlier stages of Canadian history, Toronto was once again designated a provincial capital, this time of the new Province of Ontario.

Toronto continued its remarkable growth as each decade passed. In 1879, the citizens organized the first of their Canadian National Exhibitions, a huge annual showcase of agricultural and technical wares that drew exhibitors and visitors from around the nation. In 1881, the energy of mighty Niagara Falls was harnessed to provide hydroelectric power. This guaranteed Toronto a cheap source of energy to run its rapidly expanding industries.

Continued Expansion for the Modern Age

A year later, the city began absorbing surrounding towns to create a more efficient metropolitan area. Within the next 30 years, the city doubled in size and increased its population five times over.

The twentieth century brought Toronto continued good fortune, even through the Depression of the 1930s. The city's diverse economy made it less vulnerable to the pressures that beset other cities. Toronto's industries were particularly important during the war years, further boosting prosperity. The only real problem the city had, in fact, was growth itself. This once small city had turned into a fast-growing metropolis that had not kept pace with its own success. Specifically, the city was having difficulty providing urban services, such as transportation, police, education, and housing. Many of these problems were because services required the cooperation of many towns and neighborhoods, each with different ideas and different budgets.

Thoughtful leaders believed the city and its suburbs could best be managed through a single political organization. In 1953, the Ontario provincial legislature created the Municipality of Metropolitan Toronto and established a Metro Council serving a total population of nearly 3 million people.

Toronto Today

The Toronto of today is known as the "power broker of the nation." Prosperous and ultra-modern, the city's skyline is a silhouette of banks, investment houses, publishers, and design firms. Nearly 15 percent of all Canadians live in the bustling city, and many work to produce a major part of Canada's exports. Since 1981, the average income of residents has soared, and the Toronto Stock Exchange has buzzed with constant activity.

Toronto citizens do not like having their city compared to New York, but moviemakers often use the city as a New York look-alike. More than 100 American films and television shows are produced on the streets of Toronto each year.

In the past 25 years, the city of Toronto has slowly developed a distinct identity. It has come to be known as perhaps the best example of an ideal modern city. Its streets are clean, its public transportation is well-designed, and its shiny new buildings offer many places for city dwellers to meet and relax.

The city's politics are also rather modern. Housing, and social welfare programs reflect the "liberal" attitudes of Canada in general; citizens are well-provided for. Smoking is forbidden in all public buildings. And handguns must be registered with the local government. In many ways, Toronto stands as a shining example of what a large city can be. It has learned from the mistakes of older cities and has steered its own unique course toward prosperity.

A metropolitan mounted policeman sits atop his horse in front of City Hall.

THE PEOPLE

"Toronto is the rather rapid creation of a vibrant mix of cultures that has echoes of turn-of-the-century New York City—but without the slums, crowding, disease, and tensions."

—Allan Gould, Canadian author

Young Torontonians prepare to march in the city's Santa Claus parade.

In the beginning, many of the people who settled early Toronto and the surrounding area were either Protestant English or English-Americans. The latter had sided with the king in the American Revolution and fled to Canada out of fear when their side lost. Protestant in their religious beliefs, solid and prudish, these peoples had cleared land, started farms, and established new towns and businesses. Before long they had built a stable, economically vigorous but rather unexciting society. Their new society was distinctly different from the French settlements in Quebec and the swashbuckling frontier towns to the west.

Citywide celebrations are frequent in Toronto. Here, the Kensington Karnival parade winds through the city.

New Cultures and Influences

To a significant degree, this state of affairs continued until after World War II. Since that time, there
has been a great influx of non-English peoples into
Toronto, in numbers that altered the old character of
the city. Toronto today is a mosaic of many smaller
ethnic neighborhoods, each with its own distinct
character. Indeed, a quarter of all immigrants com-
ing to Canada since the end of World War II have
chosen Toronto as their new home.

By some reports, there are as many Italians in
Toronto as in Florence, Italy, and more West Indians
than on the island of Grenada. Toronto also has the
largest gathering of Portuguese in North America

Toronto has an impressive mix of
cultures from all over the world. Of
the 3.8 million people who live in the
city, almost 70 percent of them were
born and raised somewhere else.

and the second largest community of Estonians. Other sizable groups include Chinese, Ukrainians, Germans, and eastern European Jews. According to Toronto's own census, more than 70 ethnic groups live in the city, speaking more than 100 different languages! With the growth of the city's population has come a change in Toronto's religious character. Gradually, the city has gone from being a Protestant stronghold to one that has room for many religious beliefs. While Toronto can still be called "the City of Churches," the houses of worship today are as diverse as the people they serve.

An Example of Harmony

Happily, the different groups seem to live together with uncommon cooperation and tolerance. Because of this, the city is often held up as an example of harmony to other North American cities. *Fortune* magazine, for example, called Toronto "America's newest great city," based in large part upon its civilized quality of life. And Peter Ustinov, the Russian-English actor, has described Toronto as "New York run by the Swiss."

Toronto boasts many famous hometown personalities. A significant percentage of them are names in entertainment, including Mary Pickford, one of the truly great stars of the silent film era of the movies. Other natives include Raymond Massey, a fine post-World War II actor of stage and film; Joe Shuster, the creator of *Superman;* and Norman Jewison, the highly acclaimed theater director and producer whose contemporary credits include *Fiddler on the Roof, In the Heat of the Night,* and *Moonstruck.* John Candy, the hefty funnyman of *Uncle Buck, Splash, Stripes,* and other movies is also a Torontonian.

Toronto has given the world some major medical heroes. Among them are doctors Frederick Banting and Charles Best, who discovered insulin. This hormone is involved in blood sugar regulation, and Banting and Best developed the first methods of administering the substance to diabetics. Also a

Toronto's Chinatown is a central meeting place for the city's 100,000 Chinese citizens.

Folk dancing in traditional costumes is a large part of the annual Canada Day celebration.

native of Toronto is Dr. Allen Brown, who invented Pablum, the specially balanced cereal food on which generations of babies first dined.

Glenn Gould, the classical pianist and world-famous composer, was born in Toronto in 1932.

Rich in Culture

Today's Toronto is a stimulating place to live, with education and the arts major features of the city's cultural life. In most things cultural, Toronto has long been a dominant force in its province and the

Film actress Mary Pickford was a Toronto native.

Cultures from Asia—such as Asian Indians—play a large part in Toronto's ethnic mix.

Native writer Margaret Atwood is a proud Torontonian.

nation. The first school of Canadian painters—the Group of Seven as they called themselves—appeared in Toronto in the 1920s, and succeeded for a time in establishing a distinctive Canadian style of landscape painting. With government support, Canadian novelists, poets, playwrights, dancers, and musicians have also flocked to Toronto since the twenties. Toronto is also the home of the Toronto Symphony Orchestra, the National Ballet of Canada, the Canadian Opera Company, and several resident theater groups.

A City of Recreation

Torontonians are avid sports enthusiasts, both as spectators and players. There are fine facilities both inside the city and within reasonable traveling distances outside the city limits. Toronto has several big league teams: the Toronto Blue Jays in baseball's American League; the Maple Leafs in NHL Hockey; and the Argos in the Canadian Football League. Toronto's location provides an exceptional amount of public waterfront and park acreage—8,700 acres in total. Many citizens also find time and opportunity to sail, row, scull, ski, bicycle, skate, hike, camp out, canoe, fish, and horseback ride.

Torontonians also play several amateur sports that are notably Canadian: ice hockey, curling, and lacrosse. Ice hockey was first played in Canada in 1875, when a group of students at McGill University in Montreal made a pastime of slatting a ball around

The covered Toronto SkyDome houses sporting events all year.

The beautiful marinas of the Toronto Islands are just an eight-minute trip across the bay from the downtown.

the ice. It is considered *the* national sport today. Curling originated in Scotland and involves the sliding of rounded pieces of granite over the ice, somewhat in the manner of shuffleboard. Lacrosse is a field game adopted from the Canadian Native North Americans and taken up by early French and English soldiers for amusement. A very fast game that involves a ball and sticks with nets, lacrosse tends to be even rougher than soccer or football.

The people of Toronto enjoy their sports, but they are also uncommonly hard workers the rest of the time. Their work ethic is evident in their motto, "Industry, Intelligence, Integrity." Toronto is the center of Canada's financial activities, with the headquarters of many of the nation's largest corporations located on or near Bay Street. Banking, publishing, the communications industry, filmmaking, retailing, and meat packing are centered here. Toronto is also the manufacturing headquarters of Canada. It is home to such important industries as the manufacture of electrical machinery and agricultural equipment, chemicals, newsprint, furniture, clothing, textiles, beverages, and food products.

Residents play ring hockey on Grenadier Pond in High Park.

(Opposite page)
A Toronto street musician uses instruments made from pieces of ordinary objects.

ON THE TOUR BUS

Landmarks and Special Places

Art Gallery of Ontario, 317 Dundas Street West. Houses a collection of over 15,000 works of fine art, ranging from Old Masters to contemporary works. The gallery's greatest fame, however, rests upon its huge collection of sculptures donated by the great British sculptor Henry Moore, who had a special affection for Toronto.

Black Creek Pioneer Village, Jane Street and Steeles Avenue, in suburban Downsview. This village is a living history museum assembled around the nucleus of a pioneer farm of the early 1800s. Costumed guides demonstrate all sorts of early trades and skills amidst a collection of 20 carefully restored buildings.

Casa Loma, 1 Austin Terrace. Canada's only castle, this 98-room medieval and Gothic style mansion was built around 1913 for financier Sir Henry Pellatt. Its extravagant furnishings reportedly contributed to the

Casa Loma

owner's downfall, and soon after its completion the city took it over. Casa Loma stands atop one of the few hills in Toronto.

CN (Canadian National) Tower, 301 Front Street West, close by the lakefront and harbor. At 1,815 feet (553.33 meters), this communications tower is the tallest *freestanding* tower in the world. (New York's World Trade Center is almost 500 feet shorter.) The Tower carries a host of transmission facilities, including UHF and VHF television, FM radio, and microwave transmitting stations. It opened in 1976 and became almost immediately one of the principal tourist attractions in the city, drawing an average of 1.7 million tourists every year. From its observation deck, which is reached via four glass elevators on the outside of the structure, visitors can see almost 100 miles on a clear day. The world's largest revolving restaurant is another remarkable feature of the structure.

The Tower has also drawn lots of stuntsmen: one rode a motorcycle up the 2,570 steps for a Guinness Record; another *tumbled* head over heels down the stairs in an hour and 51 minutes; two others carried a 275-pound refrigerator up the stairs in one hour and 47 seconds. And every year a thousand or more participants compete for time in climbing a somewhat shorter segment of the staircase, 1,760 steps, for charity: the current record is 8 minutes and 17 seconds!

At the foot of the Tower stands another Toronto landmark: the *SkyDome*, a multipurpose stadium with seating capacity for 56,000 spectators and the world's first fully retractable roof, home to the Toronto Blue Jays and the Argos.

Houses and Mansions

Gibson House, 5172 Yonge Street, North York. David Gibson, a Scottish-born surveyor who served in William Lyon Mackenzie's "army" in the Rebellion of 1837, built this Georgian brick house in the mid-1800s upon his return from exile in the United States. The house operates as a museum, offering daily demonstrations of pioneer crafts.

The Grange, Dundas and Beverley Streets. The home of two generations of the Boulton family, members of Toronto's old ruling elite, this Georgian building was erected about 1818. Here, many members of the Family Compact gathered regularly to discuss local affairs. This house eventually was deeded to the Art Gallery of Ontario.

Historic Fort York, Fleet Street West and Garrison Road. The first British military post established in the region, this restored fort dates back to 1793. Though many buildings were torched in the British retreat of 1813, it was immediately rebuilt. Eight of the log, stone, and brick buildings from that era remain and are the site of periodic military exhibitions and demonstrations.

Mackenzie House, 82 Bond Street. In the last years of his

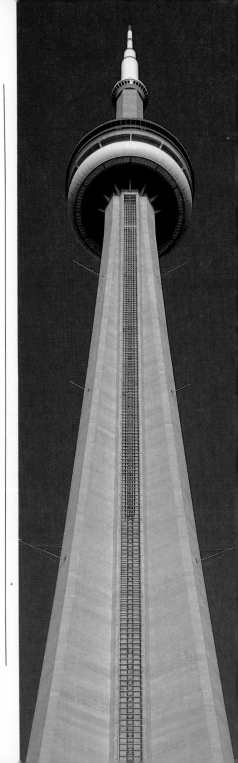

The CN Tower

The Art Gallery of Toronto

colorful life, William Lyon Mackenzie occupied this handsome Victorian house, which was bought for him by grateful admirers. Mackenzie died here on August 28, 1861, and legend has it that his ghost walks the halls by night. Torontonians revere Mackenzie as one of the founders of Canadian democracy.

Museums and Exhibits

Marine Museum, Exhibition Place. The officers' quarters of an 1841 army barracks has been rededicated to displaying the paraphernalia of Toronto's extensive maritime history, from the watercraft of the early *coureur de bois* to recent aspects of life on the St. Lawrence Seaway.

Ontario Science Centre, 770 Don Mills Road. Over 800 hands-on exhibits in this huge science and technology display; also, live demonstrations and films.

Provincial Parliament Building, Queen's Park. An imposing structure of granite and pink sandstone, this Romanesque Revival building was opened in 1893. Visitors today may observe Ontario's provincial government in action, usually from March until the end of June and again from October to mid-December; tours of the handsome interiors are available throughout the year.

Royal Ontario Museum, 100 Queens' Park. Opened in 1933, the museum has perhaps the finest collection of ancient Chinese art to be found anywhere in the world outside of China, as well as fine collections relating to life sciences, art, and archaeology.

Scadding Cabin, Exhibition Place. The oldest house in Toronto, this log cabin was built in 1794 by pioneer John Scadding, one of Governor Simcoe's staff.

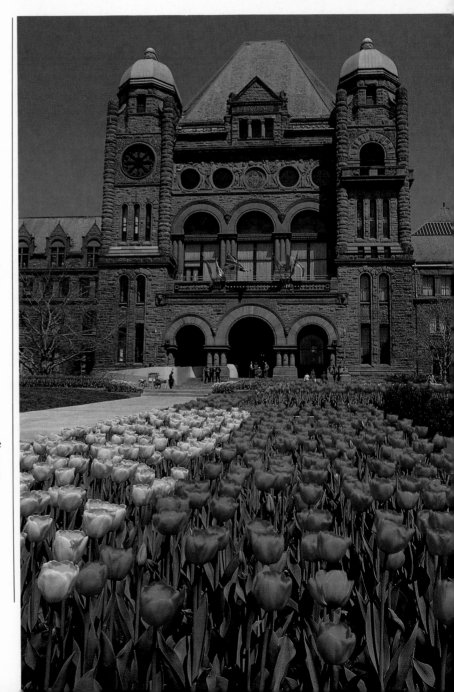

The Parliament Building

A street vendor on Queen Street

The Dinosaur Gallery at the Royal
Ontario Museum

58

St. Lawrence Hall and Market, Jarvis Street, between Front and King Streets. In the first decade after Toronto became a city, the top floor of this hall served as municipal offices and police court, the lower floor as a collection of retail markets. The municipal functions moved next door in 1844, but the markets and the history remain.

Toronto's First Post Office, 260 Adelaide Street. Together with the neighboring Bank of Upper Canada, this old post office building dates back to the early days when Toronto was known as York and the postal service was under British direction. A costumed postmaster tends to his postal duties while providing contemporary service.

Enoch Turner Schoolhouse, 106 Trinity Street. Toronto's first free schoolhouse presents displays of early city life.

Underground Toronto. The world's largest subterranean complex, this underground temperature-controlled pedestrian city stretches six blocks north and south, with much of it under the city's financial district. It was begun in 1977 and completed 10 years later. More than 1,000 shops and services, as well as hotels, restaurants, and theaters, lie along its long, twisting passageways.

University of Toronto, West of Queen's Park. The center of higher education for some 50,000 students, this university was founded in 1827. Its many buildings present a capsule history of nineteenth- and twentieth-century architectural styles.

Events

Metro International Caravan, a city-wide celebration of Toronto's ethnic diversity. A festival of arts, food, and entertainment for nine days in June.

Dominion Day, Canada's most important national holiday. Like the Fourth of July, Dominion Day is a kind of national birthday, marked with fireworks and picnics. July 1.

The National Ballet of Canada

CHRONOLOGY

1497	John Cabot lands on Canadian soil, staking claim for England.
1534	Jacques Cartier sails up the Gulf of St. Lawrence, claiming lands for France.
1608	Samuel de Champlain chooses site of Quebec for permanent French settlement.
1615	Étienne Brûlé, the first *coureur de bois,* stops at the site of the future Toronto.
1642	Montreal founded.
1689-1763	French and Indian Wars fought for control of New France territory.
1763	Treaty of Paris surrenders most of New France to England.
1760-1783	Era of northward migration to Canada by pro-Loyalist American settlers escaping the American Revolution.
1775	The American Revolution begins.
1791	Constitutional Act divides Quebec into Upper Canada and Lower Canada, each a distinct British province with its own legislative assembly.
1793	John Graves Simcoe chooses Toronto as the first permanent capital of Upper Canada, naming it York.
1812-1814	U.S. declares war on Britain and invades Canada. Fort Newark and York's Parliament buildings burned.
1815-1841	The era of the Tory Family Compact.
1827	King's College in York chartered, now the University of Toronto.
1834	York incorporated as a city named Toronto, and William Lyon Mackenzie elected its first mayor.
1837	Mackenzie's popular rebellion breaks out in Toronto and is defeated.

1839	John George Lambton's (Lord Durham) *Report on the Affairs of British North America* submitted to Queen Victoria, leading to democratic reforms.
1840	Act of Union joins Upper Canada (Ontario) and Lower Canada (Quebec) into united provinces of Canada.
1840	Sewers and gas lines installed on the main streets of Toronto.
1849	Major fire destroys much of downtown Toronto.
1851	Population of Canada West (Ontario) reaches 950,000.
1853	First Canadian railway steam engine built and operated in Toronto.
1861	First horse-drawn street cars operated as public transportation in center city.
1867	Dominion of Canada established, dividing the provinces of Canada into Ontario and Quebec and uniting them with the provinces of New Brunswick and Nova Scotia. Ottawa chosen over Toronto as national capital.
1881	Niagara Falls harnessed for hydroelectric power.
1913	Casa Loma built for financier Henry Mill Pellatt.
1949	Subway system under construction in Toronto.
1954	Metropolitan Toronto created as a political unit.
1954-1959	The St. Lawrence Seaway is constructed.
1976	CN Tower opened, becoming the dominant feature on Toronto's cityscape.
1987	Underground Toronto opened.

For Further Reading

Careless, J.M.S. and R. Craig Brown, ed. *The Canadians, 1867-1967.* St. Martin's Press, 1967.

Clark, Gerald. *Canada: The Uneasy Neighbor.* David McKay, 1965.

Ferguson, Linda. *Canada.* Charles Scribner's Sons, 1979.

Fodor's Toronto. Fodor's Travel Publications, 1987.

Fulfort, Robert. *Canada: A Celebration.* Key Porter Books, 1983.

McNaught, Kenneth. *The History of Canada.* Praeger, 1970.

Shepherd, Jenifer. *Canada.* Childrens Press, 1987.

Walz, Jay and Audrey. *Portrait of Canada.* New York Times, 1970.

Woodcock, George. *The Canadians.* Harvard University Press, 1979.

Where to Get More Information

Archives of Ontario, Ministry of Culture
  & Communications, 77 Grenville St.,
  Toronto, ON M7A 2R9

Ontario Historical Society, Toronto
  5151 Yonge St., Willowdale, On M2N
  5P5

*Metropolitan Toronto Convention &
  Visitors Association,* Queen's Quay
  West, Toronto, ON M5J 1A7

Toronto Historical Board, Historical
  Place, Stanley Barracks, Toronto, ON
  M6K 3C#

INDEX

Photo credits

Cover: © Pete Ryan/First Light Toronto; p. 4–5: © A.E. Sirulnikoff/First Light Toronto; p. 7, 12, 41, 55: © Steve Vidler/Leo de Wys, Inc.; p. 8–9: Leo de Wys, Inc.; p. 11: © J.B. Grant/Leo de Wys, Inc.; p. 13, 51 (bottom): © Ron Watts/First Light Toronto; p. 14: © Lorraine C. Parrow/First Light Toronto; p. 16–17: Private Collection; p. 19: The Bettmann Archive; p. 20, 24, 35–36: © The New York Public Library Picture Collection; p. 22: National Archives of Canada; p. 23: © Barry Dursley/First Light Toronto; p. 27: University of Michigan Library; p. 28: Royal Ontario Museum, Toronto; p. 29: Franklin Delano Roosevelt Library; p. 30, 58 (bottom): Royal Ontario Museum, Toronto; p. 33: McCord Museum of Modern Canadian History; p. 38: Private Collection; p. 42–43: © Barry Dursley/First Light Toronto; p. 44, 48, 49, 53, 57: © Gera Dillon/First Light Toronto; p. 45: © Paul von Baich/First Light Toronto; p. 47: © Dawn Goss/First Light Toronto; p. 49: The Bettmann Archive; p. 50: © Laurence Acland/courtesy Doubleday; p. 51 (top): © Jim Russell/First Light Toronto; p. 52: © Mark Burnham/First Light Toronto; p. 54: © Michael-Philip Manheim/First Light Toronto; p. 56: © Brian Milne/First Light Toronto; p. 58 (top): © Dave Prichard/First Light Toronto; p. 59: © B. Gray/The National Ballet of Canada.